GREAT CLASSICAL MUSIC
FOR VIOLIN & PIANO

25 Favorite Classical Pieces in
Intermediate Level Arrangements

ISBN 978-1-5400-8344-9

Visit Hal Leonard Online at
www.halleonard.com

World headquarters, contact:
Hal Leonard
7777 West Bluemound Road
Milwaukee, WI 53213
Email: info@halleonard.com

In Europe, contact:
Hal Leonard Europe Limited
1 Red Place
London, W1K 6PL
Email: info@halleonardeurope.com

In Australia, contact:
Hal Leonard Australia Pty. Ltd.
4 Lentara Court
Cheltenham, Victoria, 3192 Australia
Email: info@halleonard.com.au

Contents

Moonlight Sonata
(First Movement)

Ludwig van Beethoven
(1770–1827)

Habañera
from *Carmen*

Georges Bizet
(1838–1875)

Hungarian Dance No. 5

Johannes Brahms
(1833–1897)

Waltz

from *16 Waltzes*, Op. 39, No. 15

Johannes Brahms
(1833–1897)

Rêverie

Claude Debussy
(1862–1918)

Mazurka
Op. 7, No. 1

Frédéric Chopin
(1810–1849)

Dance of the Blessed Spirits
from *Orfeo*

Christoph Willibald von Gluck
(1714–1787)

Solveig's Song
from Peer Gynt Suite No. 2

Edvard Grieg
(1843–1907)

Largo
(Ombra mai fu)
from *Serse*

George Frideric Handel
(1685–1759)

Liebestraum No. 3
from *Three Liebesträume*

Franz Liszt
(1811–1886)

Spring Song

from *Songs Without Words*, Op. 62, No. 6

Felix Mendelssohn
(1809–1847)

Barcarolle
from *The Tales of Hoffman*

Jacques Offenbach
(1819–1880)

Violin Concerto No. 1
(First Movement Theme)

Niccolò Paganini
(1782–1840)

The Young Prince and the Young Princess

from *Scheherezade*

Nikolai Rimsky-Korsakov
(1844–1908)

William Tell
(Overture)

Gioachino Rossini
(1792–1868)

The Swan
from *Carnival of the Animals*

Camille Saint-Saëns
(1835–1921)

Serenade

Franz Schubert
(1797–1828)

Andante con moto

Unfinished Symphony
(First Movement Theme)

Franz Schubert
(1797–1828)

Slowly with expression

The Happy Farmer Returning Home from Work

from *Album for the Young*, Op. 68, No. 10

Robert Schumann
(1810–1856)

Of Strange Lands and People

from *Scenes from Childhood*, Op. 15, No. 1

Robert Schumann
(1810–1856)

Traumerei

from *Scenes from Childhood*, Op. 15, No. 7

Robert Schumann
(1810–1856)

Emperor Waltz

Johann Strauss II
(1825–1899)

Chanson Triste

Pyotr Il'yich Tchaikovsky
(1840–1893)

La donna è mobile
from the opera *Rigoletto*

Giuseppe Verdi
(1813–1901)

Bridal Chorus
from *Lohengrin*

Richard Wagner
(1813–1883)